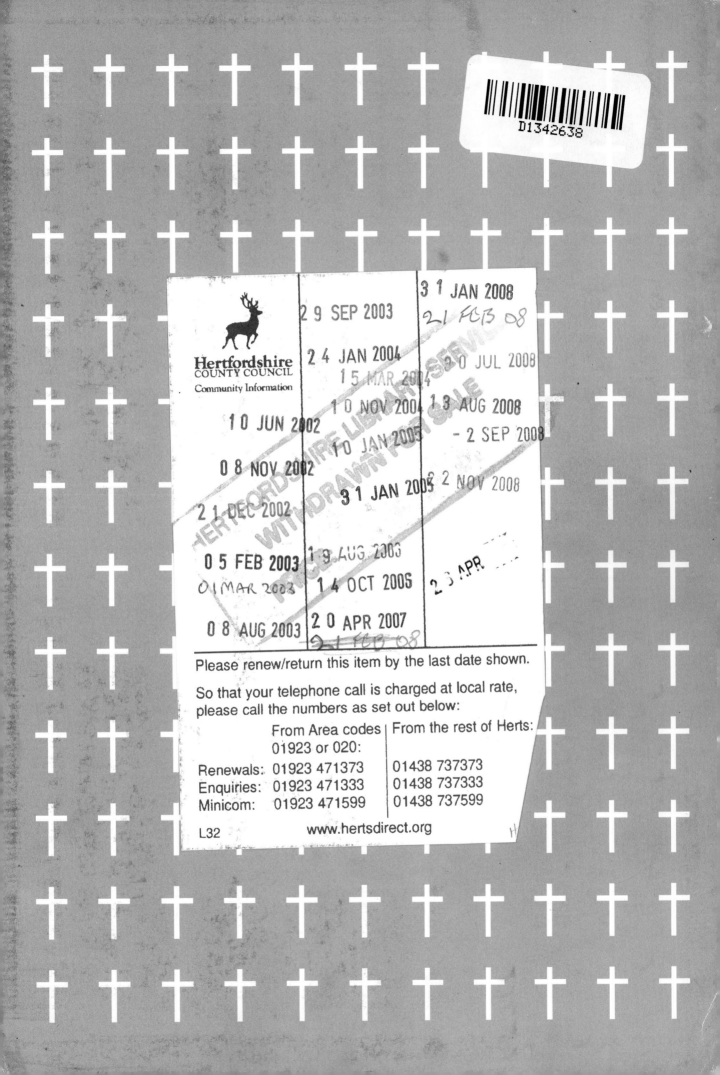

WESTERN FRONT

CAXTON EDITIONS
AN IMPRINT OF CAXTON PUBLISHING GROUP
20 BLOOMSBURY STREET, LONDON WC1 3QA

ISBN 1 84067 292 7

A COPY OF THE CIP DATA IS AVAILABLE FROM THE
BRITISH LIBRARY UPON REQUEST

DESIGNED AND PRODUCED FOR CAXTON EDITIONS
BY KEITH POINTING DESIGN CONSULTANCY

REPROGRAPHICS BY GA GRAPHICS.
PRINTED AND BOUND IN
SINGAPORE BY APP PRINTING

ACKNOWLEDGMENTS
THE IMPERIAL WAR MUSEUM

COPY EDITOR
ROSANNA NEGROTTI

DESIGN ASSISTANCE AND MAPS
JOHN BATHO

THE
WESTERN
FRONT

A PICTORIAL HISTORY

TEXT BY
DAVID RAY

CAXTON EDITIONS

CONTENTS

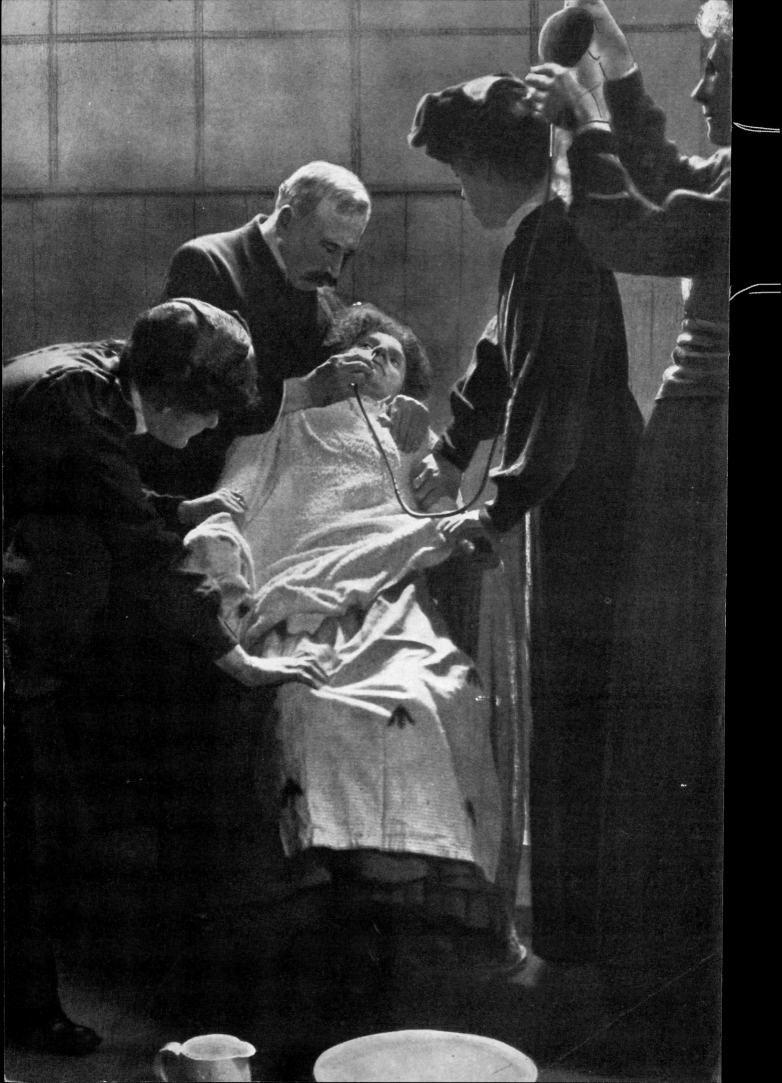

CHAPTER ONE

Origins

T HE FIRST HALF OF 1914 was eventful. Suffragettes were being arrested after assaults on politicians with dog-whips, slashing National Gallery paintings and burning down the Britannia Pier at Great Yarmouth. England achieved a Rugby Football grand slam culminating in a huge 39-13 victory in Paris. America was involved in a war with Mexico and there was simmering unrest in Ireland. On 25 June the British fleet paid a courtesy visit to Kiel. The White Ensign flew alongside the Imperial Eagle and the Kaiser was entertained on board the flagship *King George V*. Yet there was growing tension. Continental Europe was a conflict ready to happen. A mixture of nationalism, alliances, mutual distrust, militarism and economic rivalry merely needed a spark to ignite an already primed tinderbox.

LEFT: Suffragette prisoner on a hunger strike being force-fed by prison authorities, 1912.

On 28 June, Archduke Franz Ferdinand and his wife visited Sarajevo. The heir to the Austro-Hungarian Empire was shot by a nineteen-year-old Serb anarchist. The ensuing ultimatum, declarations and mobilisations were many and complex. Due to the logistics of 1914, mobilisation really meant war. Germany and Austria were allies; Britain was concerned at Germany's naval development and supported Belgian neutrality. France was allied to Russia and highly suspicious of the German-Austrian-Italian alliance. Austro-Hungary sent Serbia humiliating demands on 23 July; Russia mobilised, followed by France. Germany declared war on France. Germany felt encircled; a war on two fronts would fail unless a pre-emptive strike was planned. Later there would be designs on French and British colonies and the desire to carve out an empire to the east.

RIGHT: Queen Victoria, 1900.

Tsar Nicholas II and family, c1900.

Britain declared war on Germany on 4 August. The main reason was to uphold the balance of power in Europe and to 'resist the complete ascending of Germany in Europe.' There had been no conflict between the Great Powers for forty years. The populations of France, Germany and Britain were excited, and the general view was that there would be some great battles with everything concluded by Christmas. It would be, by Christmas 1918.

LEFT: Photographed a few minutes before their death, the Archduke Franz Ferdinand and his wife in Sarajevo, on 28 June 1914.

OVERLEAF: The bomb-thrower hustled into custody after the assassination at Sarajevo, 1914.

FOLLOWING PAGE: Recruits at the Whitehall Recruiting Office, August 1914. Britain's declaration of War on Germany on 4 August was greeted for the most part with popular enthusiasm, and resulted in a rush of men to enlist.

ABOVE: Men of the North Lancs regiment cheering after being ordered to the trenches.

CHAPTER TWO

Initial Moves

In 1914, NEARLY ALL European nations were monarchies. The Kaiser's mother was English and his uncle was King Edward VII, but he had no time for the English. Britain's Navy with sixty-eight battleships and cruisers dominated the seas, while Germany's army was seven times that of Britain's. The British were in khaki; the Germans in field-grey, complete with *pickelhaube* and the French still wore red trousers, blue coats and white gloves. Tin helmets were something for the future. The British land forces were small but what became known as that 'contemptible little army' was probably the most efficient in the world. The Russian army was large with over four million men, but it was poorly organised.

LEFT: The Kaiser, c1905.

Technical improvements in weaponry had escalated in the late nineteenth century. The machine-gun was already in service by the 1890s and the rifle was vastly superior to anything previously used by combatants. Rifled and breech-loaded artillery merely added weight to the power of defence in a future war.

German military theory could be traced back to von Clausewitz in the 1830s. Rapid mobility, mass warfare and short duration dominated thinking and the Schlieffen plan attempted to put this into practice. A swift advance westwards through Luxembourg and Belgium would be followed by a southerly sweep of their five armies to engulf Paris. A six-week campaign was envisaged. The Germans relied on highly trained officers and NCOs, a large number of reserve troops and an army conveniently camped on the Belgian border.

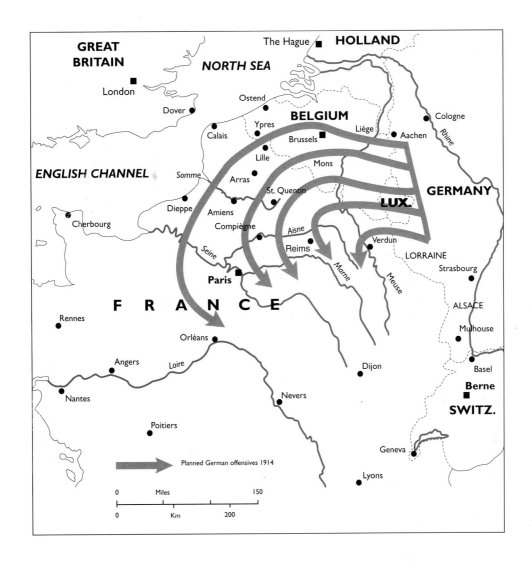

ABOVE: The Schlieffen plan.

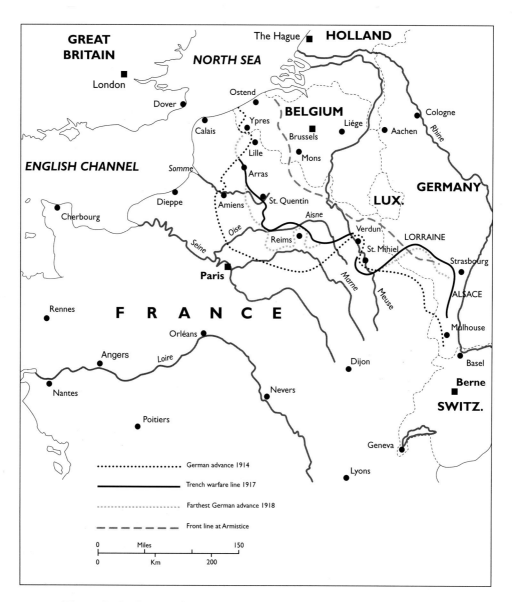

ABOVE: The whole front.

Belgium was a 'minnow' amongst its neighbours. Initially, its troops delayed the German advance but the juggernaut rolled on. Liège and Brussels were taken and during late August the Germans streamed into France. The British Expeditionary Force to the north slowed the advance at Mons on 23 and then on 26 August at Le Cateau, and the French caused problems in the Ardennes. The German supply lines became stretched to the limit but they were only fifty kilometres from Paris. The Battle of the Maine that followed was a turning point. The Schlieffen plan was shelved, the German General Moltke displayed indecision and lack of nerve, the Germans were committed to war on two fronts and trench warfare began at the following Battle of the Aisne. A series of attempted out-flanking movements to the north led to the so-called 'race to the sea'. This set the scene for static lines that became the forerunner of trench warfare. The concept of a short war disappeared. The name of Ypres now entered the frame.

CHAPTER THREE

How the Nations Lined Up

It is difficult today to appreciate the paranoia, jingoism and numbers involved in the military at that time. Vast areas of the world were controlled by Britain, France, Belgium, Holland and Portugal. The USA hardly featured in the strategic equation. Only four years earlier Blériot had managed to cross the Channel in what today looks like a Heath Robinson invention.

Britain had realised that an army might be needed on the continent as well as in some far-flung colony. The Royal Navy was very much the

LEFT: The 4th Battalion of the Worcestershire Regiment (29th Division), marching to the trenches. Acheux, 28 June 1918.

'senior service' however, and the High Command still put most of their faith in the cavalry. One million horses were taken to the Western Front by the British. Sixty-two thousand got back. At least the British generals had had recent experience of war, and the infantry had been forced to improve its efficiency in the South African War. Conscription for single men would be introduced in January 1915, and four months later, for married men aged eighteen to forty-five.

Right up to the age of forty-five, German males were also involved in the military whether it was in training, the *landwehr* (Home Guard), the *landsturm* (Territorials) or the wonderfully named Ersatz Reserve. Their large numerical and tactical superiority was tempered by an element of inflexibility; repetitious practice tended to blunt Germanic efficiency. In France, offensive tactics and élan dominated military thought and training. The French did not rate the machine-gun in the early days. They were at a demographic disadvantage to the Germans but they could rely on sizeable numbers of colonial troops such as the Zouaves from Morocco and the Turcos from Algeria.

The next four years would see a transformation in warfare on land, at sea and in the air. 'The war to end all wars', the Great War or the first 'total' war would change things for evermore. Names like Passchendaele and the Verdun forts would come to symbolise something dreadful, the USA would emerge on the world stage and Europe would set itself up for an even longer, global conflict twenty years later.

OVERLEAF: Annamites, French Colonial Marine Infantry from Cochin, China, May 1916.

CHAPTER FOUR

The First Battle of Ypres and the Christmas Truce

ONCE THE LINES HAD been solidified, the Belgian town of Ypres became strategically critical to both sides. If Ypres fell it was believed the Channel ports would quickly be captured. The First Battle of Ypres commenced on 19 September 1914. The Germans put young volunteers into this sector and the result became known as 'The Massacre of the Innocents'. It was a mixture of traditional and trench warfare. The Germans next attacked between Messines and Gheluvelt; the British were pushed off the Messines ridge and by the end of the year, the Germans held virtually all the high ground on three sides of

LEFT: British troops arriving on leave at a London terminus.

Ypres. Both sides had lost the majority of their pre-war regulars. In fact, the Germans never realised how near they came to taking Ypres. The remnants of the 2nd Worcestershires – a mere 230 men – repelled the Prussian Guard on 11 November and plugged the gap. The Germans had missed their chance but it was to be three more long years before the British took the Messines ridge. By 22 November the battle was over. The British Expeditionary Force had lost 50,000 men, the Germans nearer to 100,000. The Western Front stretched from the Channel to the borders of Switzerland.

At some sectors on the new front line, unofficial truces occurred on Christmas Day 1914. Photographs of the two sides mixing in no man's land were taken, mementoes were exchanged and for the first and last time, peace and brotherhood descended on western Flanders. At

RIGHT: German advance in 1914.

Ploegsteert, the London Rifle Regiment warily fraternised. One British soldier met his German barber from High Holborn and an impromptu short-back-and-sides took place between the trenches. The High Command was furious at this worrying trend and strict orders about such activity in the future were issued. Next morning the shelling and shooting resumed.

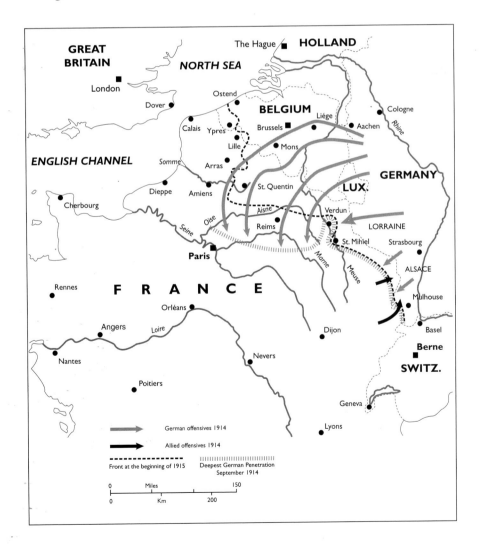

CHAPTER FIVE

Trench Life

If ANYTHING SUMS UP the Western Front it's trench warfare. Trenches were nothing new; they had even been used in the American Civil War. However, it was the length and longevity of the system that made this war so unusual. By December, a vast network stretched over 600km. Some sections hardly moved in four years. Only the Iran-Iraq conflict of the 1980s comes close. It's difficult for someone today to comprehend the conditions the troops endured in these gruesome holes. The front-line soldiers often only got what was left after rations had been pilfered or sold. Hot meals were rare, and the hardships included mud, rats, lice and of course an enemy that might be only

LEFT: Officers of the 12th Royal Irish Rifles wading through the mud of a fallen-in communication trench, the result of a thaw after weeks of snow and frost. They had recently taken over from the French 6th Division. Essigny, 7 February 1918.

twenty-five metres away. There was little romance in this war. Rats were detested by both sides; they carried disease and grew fat and sluggish on the rich pickings of German, French and British alike in no man's land. On Vimy Ridge, the forward trenches were so close a hand grenade could be lobbed with devastating effect. On the positive side, there were trench cats, pet dogs and mascots such as the goat of the Royal Scots. Dogs were used as draught animals by the Belgians, and the British used them for carrying messages and taking wire for communications between trenches.

Dugouts and walls provided sleeping quarters. The Germans went deeper and their accommodation was almost luxurious compared to the French and British slums. They even had wallpaper and beds with springs. The Germans intended to stay, and their units remained longer in a sector. By and large the British were more active than the French while the Prussians had a reputation for more action than the Bavarians.

'Stand To' started the day followed by rudimentary ablutions. Trench foot – a form of gangrene, and trench fever – an illness akin to flu or typhoid – were two of the hazards of life in this environment. Thousands of troops got a 'Blighty', a wound that meant a return to Britain. Self-inflicted Blighties could lead to a court martial. Other such offences included sleeping on-duty and casting-away arms. In fact men fell asleep standing up, rewiring, filling sand bags and marching. The thought of yet another meal of bully beef and Ticklers' Plum or Apricot jam with a rock-hard biscuit thrown in did not do a lot for company morale. The strawberry jam tins rarely reached the front trenches unless the label had accidentally come off. In 1940 part of the British army was billeted at Fampoux near Arras on the Hindenburg line of World War I. In an old trench, they discovered a case of tins of Fray Bentos corned beef. These were eaten with no ill effects. Regimental pride was a key factor in explaining why the British Army as a whole was the only one not to mutiny. Alcohol, usually rum, a dark sense of humour and mail from home all helped to sustain morale.

For most of the conflict defences proved too strong for attacks. The rifle and bayonet with cosh, knuckle-duster and grenade had their place in trench raids, but the heavy machine-guns, gas and artillery were the masters of the battlefield. The Tommy lived in the Lambeth Road, Westminster Bridge Road and Hyde Park Corner. Livelier sectors had more pertinent names such as Windy Corner at Givenchy and Hellfire and Shrapnel Corners at Ypres.

OVERLEAF: British troops receiving dinner rations from field kitchens, Ancre area of the Somme, October 1916. Hot food was not supplied to front-line soldiers until late 1915, and even then was by no means a regular occurrence.

The Times, – 3 FEBRUARY 1915

LIFE IN A DUGOUT: an officer at the front writes:

'The damp has got into my pockets. I am wet from head to heel. My hands are caked in mud; I am wet through, and have nowhere a chance to dry myself. Everything and every pocket is ruined, and my money is nothing but a lump of coloured paper. I have tried to dry the lead pencil I am writing with by candlelight in my dugout, but it is no use. The water is trickling down the walls and gives me a shower bath all the time. My breeches are thick with mud. I don't suppose even my mother would recognise me at this minute. I have tried in vain to dry my hands. I have blown on them and held them round the candle, but it is no good. They are inches deep in mud. My revolver case has turned into putty, and my muffler is more like a mud pie than anything else. The paper I am writing on I found round some chocolate in my dugout. Somehow it had kept dry. My watch has stopped at five, as the wet and

mud have penetrated it. I have lived on chocolate all day long, and I am going into a cellar near here to get something to eat whenever I can be relieved. This cellar belongs to a ruined farm that has not a wall standing.

All day long we have heard the swish of the shells overhead and seen them fall only a few yards away and tear up and rend tremendous holes in the ground. I have just waded through our trenches, which have fallen to pieces and are filling with mud and water, parapets falling down and all the dugouts collapsing; the men standing shivering in the bitter wind on sentry duty, others huddled together trying to keep warm, but wet and grimy and caked in mud.

Am I a human being? I ask myself. I am gradually getting cold and chilled all through and will, to keep circulation going, be forced to go round my sentries to see if they are all standing by. We have not slept for nights and it is hard for everyone. I am cheerful and have a laugh ready for all my men. They have been good to me, and it is marvellous how good they are and how little grumbling there is. I dug one of my men out of the mud yesterday. I thought we had lost him, as it took one and a half hours to dig him out, but I am glad to say we pulled him round and he is quite fit again. Last night I fell into a trench full of water, and the men kept a little box full of wood burning near me all night long and brought me hot tea. They are fine and have worked splendidly all the time.'

OVERLEAF: A sentry and sleeping soldiers in a front-line trench at Ovillers-la-Boiselle on the Somme, July 1916. In this photograph one man crouches on the fire-step while his comrades rest but with weapons at the ready. 'A' company, 11th Cheshire Regiment.

FOLLOWING PAGE: Men of the York and Lancaster Regiment in the trenches on the 62nd Division front (Oppy-Gavrelle). A machine-gun mounted for anti-aircraft firing, 13 January 1918.

CHAPTER SIX

Artillery: the Role of the Big Gun

A TYPICAL BRITISH TRENCH system had three lines: front, support and reserve. The trenches were a series of traverses to give greater protection, particularly if part of the trench was taken by the enemy. There could be as much as 150m between the main and communication trenches linking them. Observation posts were placed just into no man's land, which was traditionally festooned with barbed wire. There would be a strong point to the rear and the Lewis, Maxim or Hotchkiss machine-gun positions, kings of the defence strategy, would dominate the ground. With all these weapons and impediments, and the Germans normally holding most of the high ground, frontal attacks would appear to be suicidal.

LEFT: Eight-inch Mark V howitzers of the 19th Siege Battery R.G.A. in action in the Fricourt-Mametz Valley, August 1916.

There was approximate parity in artillery at the outbreak of war, but the German howitzers dwarfed the British and French field pieces. Some of the Big Berthas were mounted on railway lines and had a range of over 40km. High explosives proved more effective than shrapnel shells but a frustrating factor was the rudimentary back-up of radio, telephone and aircraft spotting. Artillery got heavier and the barrages increased in length and intensity prior to assaults. The problem for the Allies was that the Germans were always deeper than expected, the protracted bombardment often 'gave the game away' and it left a very difficult terrain across which the infantry had to advance. The Germans' 'defence in depth', up to 7km in places, also reduced the impact of the barrage. By 1918, the Germans were using high-explosive, gas and smoke shells at selected targets for limited periods. The gains were large. Field telephones, flash-spotting and improved aircraft were some of the refinements in the artillery war.

RIGHT: Canadian troops surrounded by trench mortar bombs.

LEFT: Battle of Pilckem Ridge. Allied soldiers jacking and hauling an 18-pounder gun out of the mud. North of Ypres, 2 August 1917.

OVERLEAF: The ruins of Lens, 27 October 1918. Lens was under German occupation from October 1914 until 2 October 1918. Before withdrawing, the Germans flooded the coal mines which they had worked by forced civilian labour during their four-year occupation.

CHAPTER SEVEN

Close-Quarter Conflict and Medical Services

It would be wrong to believe that there was continuous activity in all sectors throughout the war. However, observation and sniping were important elements of trench life. Sniping positions varied; craters, fake trees and lying under garbage were all used. Snipers usually worked in pairs with rifle and binoculars. The Germans, spending longer in a sector, had the advantage, as the pairs became expert in the lie of the land and enemy routine. There was also a seasonal element to the fighting; some sectors went into virtual hibernation over the winter months.

LEFT: Rifle with periscope butt in use in the front line, Le Bois du Centre, Pont-Arcy, Aisne, 20 August, 1915.

No man's land was normally a 'no go area' unless it was intrusion by night. Patrolling to discover as much as possible about the enemy was carried on by both sides. The attitude was normally 'live and let live' if both sides had men out. But sometimes groups met between the wire and the result was a dash for the trenches and fire from both sides. Capturing an enemy was a major coup, and having control over no man's land was considered important by the British. Taking enemy positions was not the objective; it was more about morale and intelligence.

OVERLEAF: Canadian stretcher party wearing gas masks, bringing in the wounded. Domart, 9 August 1918.

FOLLOWING PAGE: Battle of Estaires. A line of men blinded by tear gas at an Advanced Dressing Station near Bethune, 10 April 1918. Each man has his hand on the shoulder of the man in front of him.

Tunnels and mines also became integral parts of trench life. By July 1916, 25,000 men were engaged in such operations. Camouflets were used to destroy German counter-mining. Conditions were normally foul. On occasions both sets of sappers were within a metre or two of each other and conversations could be heard. There were underground listening posts and on Vimy Ridge tunnels were built into the chalk, to bring the troops to the front line and get the wounded to the rear.

Chemical warfare appeared as early as October 1914. Chlorine gas was used by the Germans in 1915. Initially surprise and terror led to ground being gained. Crude masks of cotton dipped in bicarbonate of soda were gradually refined so that by 1918, proper masks with respirators were in use by both sides. In the early days the wind had to be in the right direction. Later gas was delivered by shells and the introduction of

prussic acid, mustard gas and phosgene (five times more deadly than chlorine) added variety to this most unpleasant method of warfare. Flame-throwers could reach a range of 35m but they were used primarily as 'shock' weapons.

Brandhoek New Military Cemetery, between Ypres and Poperinge, contains a unique grave. Captain Noel G. Chavasse was one of those brave men in the Royal Army Medical Corps. Chavasse is also one of only three double Victoria Cross holders and the only one to win both medals along with an MC in World War I. When studying the Western Front one tends to think of those who died and those very elderly veterans interviewed in the 1980s and 1990s. The wounded rarely get a mention.

The traditional route was Regimental Aid Post, Divisional Dressing Station to Casualty Clearing Station. Major surgery would be available at the last-named, normally well behind the range of enemy artillery. Serious cases were moved to one of the Base hospitals. At the height of battle, the wounded would lie in the open and later the surgeons had to be highly selective. Infection was exacerbated by high-explosive shells. Amputations and antiseptics were the order of the day. Blindness was a common problem in 1918 as mustard gas was used with increased vigour. Shell-shock was assumed to be cowardice for much of the war. Counselling hadn't been invented yet.

RIGHT: This dummy was used at the Camouflage School in Kensington Gardens to give an idea of a device made use of by the Germans on different parts of the front. Figures were made to appear like British soldiers by dressing dummies in captured khaki. They were placed in no man's land and, by means of a cord, an arm was raised as if for assistance. Sometimes the body was made to sit up. Generally the head was bound up in bandages. The idea was to get the British to effect a 'rescue'.

CHAPTER EIGHT

1915: stalemate

1915 BOILED DOWN to a series of French and British attacks to weaken the enemy lines. 'Papa' Joffre, the French Commander-in-Chief, believed trench warfare was a temporary aberration. The result was tens of thousands of casualties and gains of mere metres on the ground. On 10 March, the British attacked at Neuve Chapelle. The initial assault was successful, but shells were at a premium and the reserve forces were slow to move up. The Germans had time to regroup, both sides lost around twelve thousand and the moment was lost. On 22 April, the Germans released chlorine gas and the Second Battle of Ypres was under way. A

LEFT: 2nd Battalion Royal Scots Fusiliers in the trenches at La Boutillerie, Winter 1914-1915. 7th Division. Note use of loophole for rifles.

16km-wide salient was reduced to 5km and Ypres was pulverised. Yet the Germans failed to capitalise on the gas attack and the Allies were quick to adopt this new and gruesome weapon.

To the south the Germans held the imposing Vimy Ridge between Lens and Arras. To take pressure off the Russians to the east, the French attacked on 9 May and again, the initial assault was successful. But once more, reserves didn't materialise. This will be a common theme. No breakthrough and the slogging match continued. The Allies came to the conclusion that a greater artillery barrage was needed before future attacks. For the next three months, Kitchener's volunteers began to arrive in Belgian and France. On 25 September the French and British attacked, the former in Artois and Champagne, the latter at Loos. In Champagne the French used poison gas, took twenty-five thousand prisoners but only made limited gains. There was a similar story in Artois. The British used gas at Loos for the first time but yet again reserves were too detached and the two raw divisions in the initial assault didn't help. Later battles tend to mask the losses at Loos. Nearly twenty-one thousand British names of those who were never recovered are carved on the Loos memorial. It was back to the drawing board.

OVERLEAF: A gas sentry ringing an alarm at Fleurbaix, 15 miles south of Ypres, June 1916. Gas was first used on the Western Front by the Germans during the Second Battle of Ypres in April 1915. Chlorine was the first gas to be employed, followed by phosgene in December of that year. Various warning signals were used in the trenches, including bells and rattles. The soldier in the photograph is wearing the hypo or tube helmet which was used from late 1915 until the end of 1916.

CHAPTER NINE

The War at Sea

W ITH SOME DEGREE OF accuracy it could be said that World War I saw Britannia ruling the waves and Germany ruling under the waves. Submarines and mines were the effective maritime weapons of this conflict. By 1918, Britain had mined the Straits of Dover and from Norway to the Orkneys. Lord Kitchener, the founder of the volunteer army, had drowned after the *Hampshire* had hit a mine. Vast, static armies could only be fed from home. Hence the importance of transport and, for Britain and Germany, ships with supplies from allies, colonies and neutrals. By 1917 a quarter of ships leaving British ports were being sunk. Lloyd George and the admirals debated long and hard about the use of the convoy system., which Lloyd George favoured. Lloyd George eventually won the argument and once the convoy system was established losses plummeted to one per cent.

LEFT: Admiral Sir David Beatty, Commander-in-Chief of the British Fleet, photographed in 1918.

The two major factors in the eventual Allied victory were the sinking of the *Lusitania* with many American lives lost and the gradually perfected blockade of Germany's ports 'at a distance'. The former hastened America's entry into the war and the latter led to the tumbling of morale in Germany and amongst her troops.

There were skirmishes around the globe. British submarines caused havoc in the Baltic and Sea of Marmara, the Zeebrugge raid was a brilliant operation but tactically had little to commend it and several towns on the east coast of England were shelled. Other than the Battle of the Falklands in 1915, the only major encounter was in Jutland in May 1916. Two hundred and fifty ships were involved; the result was inconclusive. Britain lost more vessels but the Germans returned home and were rarely seen again. They turned their attention to the production of U-boats.

RIGHT: Field Marshal Lord Kitchener, photographed in 1916.

LEFT: A Naval airship escorting a convoy.

OVERLEAF: The crew of a German UC-1 class submarine on deck. Introduced in 1915, the submarines of this class were employed mainly on minelaying duties and carried up to twelve mines. German submarines sank 1,845,000 tons of Allied and neutral shipping between February and April 1917.

CHAPTER TEN

1916: Verdun

To look at the British sector of the Western Front in isolation would be misleading; the French sector, the Italian and Eastern fronts form parts of a whole. The two huge battles of 1916 are interlinked and it started with Erich von Falkenhayn, Chief of the German general staff, getting his retaliation in first. It was a rare example of the Germans taking the offensive. His target was Verdun, up to then a relative backwater on the front. Whether he ever intended to 'bleed France white' through his attacks remains open to debate. The city held an almost mythical quality in the hearts of the French. The plan was to lure the bulk of the French forces to defend the city. In early 1916 it was poorly defended and the Germans initially held a five-to-one advantage in infantry.

LEFT: German troops in a shell hole. Western Front.

Forts dominated the ridges and hills but many French guns had been moved north. A fearsome barrage on 21 February by fourteen hundred artillery pieces, including thirteen 'Big Bertha' mortars, preceded the attack under Crown Prince Wilhelm's Fifth Army. However, this was no mass attack, rather a series of cautious fighting patrols with the new horror weapon: flame-throwers. The fighting within the forts defending Verdun almost defies description. Hand-to-hand fighting in black tunnels, thirsty men licking condensation from the walls and burials in pits of quicklime pulled the warfare to new depths. Soldiers ate decaying horses and shot themselves.

Defending Verdun was as much a political as a military decision. Pétain was appointed to defend the city and he declared he would hold the city whatever the cost. Almost immediately, the key Fort Douaumont was captured on 25 February. A mere ten German pioneers under Sergeant Felix Kunze had infiltrated the fort and church bells rang out in celebration across Germany. Pétain's 'ils ne passeront pas' fanatical counter-attacks and round-the-clock use of the Voie Sacrée saved the city. This lifeline pumped fresh blood into the sector where it immediately haemorrhaged. Each week three thousand trucks carrying fifty thousand tons of munitions and ninety thousand men were brought up this narrow artery.

The next German offensive was to the north at Mort Homme and Hill 304, followed by the capture of Fort de Vaux on 7 June. At one point the Germans suffered 2,678 casualties for 60m of underground corridor. The Crown Prince's forces reached the outer defences of Fort Souville using phosgene gas and here they ground to a halt. German morale was low and the quality of the fresh troops was declining by the day. The French re-took Douaumont with nearly seven thousand prisoners and by November the Germans had abandoned Fort de Vaux. The battle ended on 18 December. A total of six hundred thousand casualties meant the French and German armies were never the same again. This 'mincing machine' had reduced the whole area to a crater-covered wasteland. Nine villages had been wiped off the face of the earth forever. If anyone wants to see the results of this awful battle they merely have to go to the back of the heart-rending ossuary on Douaumont ridge. The majority of the French army had been through the Verdun experience and it haunted the nation for decades to come. It led directly to the building of the Maginot line prior to World War II. Meanwhile an equally colossal clash had been taking place some 180km to the north-west.

ABOVE: French troops of the 'Iron Division', advancing towards a German position, 1916.

OVERLEAF: A Mark I Tank (C.19 'Clan Leslie'), Chimpanzee Valley, 15 September 1916 (tanks first went into action on that day).

FOLLOWING PAGE: Battle of Flers-Courcelette. German prisoners bringing in wounded, near Ginchy, 15 September 1916.

CHAPTER ELEVEN

1916: the Somme

FROM THE BATTLE OF THE SOMME in the second half of 1916, the British Army took the dominant role for the Allies on the Western Front. The few remaining members of the BEF, Territorials and the New Army had burgeoned in France and Belgium. Yet they were inexperienced compared to their opposite numbers; the Germans took care to keep officer casualties to a minimum and they had extensive knowledge of the Somme sector. To take the pressure off Verdun, Field Marshal Sir Douglas Haig's plan was to attack north-east, centred on Albert and targeted on Bapaume. Sir Henry Rawlinson, commanding

LEFT: The remains of a German soldier at Beamont Hamel, November 1916. Britain lost her army of volunteers in the trench battles north of the River Somme in late 1916. The total British, French and German casualties in the region were 1,200,000 killed, wounded or captured.

the Fourth Army, remained unconvinced that all objectives would be reached by the end of day one. There were no real strategic objectives but it was the most convenient point where the French and British sectors met.

Morale at soldier level was high, and there were reassurances that a massive bombardment would mean a walkover through the German lines. Four hundred and fifty-five heavy guns on a 30km front sounded impressive, but many shells proved to be 'duds' and over half were shrapnel-based which failed to destroy trenches or barbed wire. With the belief that the enemy would be liquidated and that a volunteer army couldn't handle sophisticated tactics, orders were given for the soldiers to advance in lines at walking pace. Faulty British security meant the Germans were ready and the bombardment pinpointed the attack times to the Germans.

After six days of constant shelling, sixty thousand British soldiers climbed out of their trenches laden down with everything from spades and gas masks to grenades and two hundred rounds of ammunition. The Germans emerged from their deep bunkers, set up their machine-guns and the result was carnage. By late afternoon there were close on sixty thousand casualties with a third dead, and most had fallen in the first hour of the so-called advance. Later waves of soldiers could hardly get over the British dead and wounded. Some of the first wave were shot as further waves hadn't expected some German strong points to have been taken; some were killed by the British barrage. The Royal Inniskillins advanced over a kilometre and took the Swabian Redoubt. Decimation of officers and wretched communications meant no consolidation and all the ground was lost. The only notable success was in the south. The British advanced to Montauban and the French, south of the Somme, made ground south-west of Péronne.

A second 'mincing machine' had been created. 1 July 1916 remains the worst day ever for British military casualties. Was Haig a 'butcher' who was playing the numbers game, or a far-sighted leader who would eventually deliver victory for the Allies? The 'lions led by donkeys' view is still being debated today, but the 'donkeys' weren't restricted to the British side – the Germans adopted exactly the same approach. Why were the same tactics used again and again, by both sides, with so little obvious success? What were the alternatives? Only in Britain is there still almost universal condemnation of the tactics and ability of the High Command.

On 14 July, another twenty thousand men attacked at dawn in the Delville, High and Bazentin-le-Petit woods. Cavalry was still being used in reserve. The attacks turned into another slogging match, but the

Allies had learnt that a 'creeping barrage' was more effective and by the end of the month the Germans had lost one hundred and sixty thousand men. At this stage another refinement in weaponry was introduced. On 15 September, eighteen Mark I tanks out of an original forty-nine sent to France, supported an attack on Flers and Courcelette. The element of surprise was total. Yet many broke down or were knocked out. By evening most were scattered or lost. Thiepval fell a week later but no major breakthrough had occurred. Haig had wanted to use tanks immediately; Churchill wanted to wait until a decisive number could be put into action.

Dreadful weather postponed activity but on 13 November, under cover of mine-blowing and morning fog, Beaucourt and Beaumont Hamel were taken. The British settled for these gains and on 19 November the

battle was closed down. The furthest gain could be walked over in a couple of hours. For concentrated carnage Verdun was the worst engagement but in terms of numbers, the Somme takes pole position. Two-thirds of the six hundred and twenty thousand Allied casualties had been British; the German numbers were probably over six hundred thousand as well. The German Army had suffered a crucial mauling and the British Army adopted a grim determination that was to get them through 1917. The two battles of 1916 also saw the fall of Joffre, Falkenhayn and Asquith. Well over three million women were now being employed in Britain.

LEFT: French troops on offensive manoeuvres in the Somme, 1916.

RIGHT: A British tank, 1917. Tanks were introduced in 1916, an advancement in weaponry which surprised the enemy.

LEFT: The British Front in Flanders.

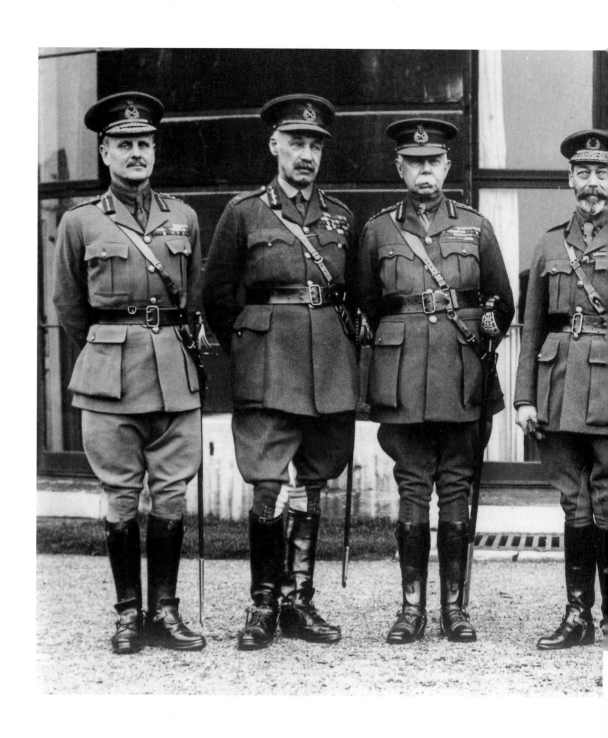

ABOVE: *Left to right*: Sir William Birdwood, Sir Henry Rawlinson, Sir Hubert Plumer, H.M. The King, Sir Douglas Haig, Sir Henry Horne, Sir Julian Byng, at Buckingham Palace, 19 December 1918.

OVERLEAF: Still from the battle of the Somme, 1916.

FOLLOWING PAGE: A gas attack at Carnoy-Montauban on the Somme, June 1916. Montauban, which was in German hands, can be seen in the top left-hand corner and Carnoy, behind the British lines, in the bottom right-hand of the corner. The gas is being released by the 18th Division as part of the preparation for the Somme offensive.

CHAPTER TWELVE

The War in the Air

INITIALLY PLANES WERE considered for nothing more than reconnaissance. Troops on the ground had a love/hate relationship with these men in the air. It was not unknown for infantry to take pot shots at planes irrespective of their markings. The combatants made huge strides in the technology of this new form of warfare. The French came up with a machine-gun that could work without shredding the propeller. The Germans had produced a monoplane by the end of 1915. Fighter tactics got more and more sophisticated – coming out of the sun, hunting in pairs and, by 1917, using large formations. After German supremacy the Allies began to gain the upper hand with improved machines such as the Sopwith Camel.

LEFT: Baron Manfred von Richthofen, known as 'The Red Baron' because he flew an all-red machine, photographed just after landing from a combat flight in his early Fokker E2. He was shot down near Sailly-le-Sec by Captain A. R. Brown, a Canadian, on 21 April 1918.

Aircraft fought aircraft and they began to be used against ground troops in 1917. The arrival of the Americans tilted the air conflict decidedly towards the Allies. Zeppelin and Gotha raids over England shook the nation. In 1918 British planes were dropping bombs over Germany. Guynemer, Mannock, Ball and von Richthofen became household names. These men were often heavily decorated but survival rates were measured in weeks rather than months. Major McCudden had won the VC, DSO and bar, DFC and bar, and MM by the time he was killed at the age of 23.

RIGHT: De Havilland 5, a single-seat fighter with 110h.p. Le Rhone engine. OVERLEAF: Sopwith F1 Camel, 130h.p. Clerget 9-Bc engine. Single-seat fighting scout. Aircraft of No. 203 squadron, R.A.F., after a forced landing at Noyelle-sur-L'Escaut, 8 October 1918.

CHAPTER THIRTEEN

The War at Home

ONLY A FEW PEOPLE thought the war would last long. Lord Kitchener, the highly regarded hero of the Sudan and South Africa, told the people to prepare for three years of hostilities and began to raise a huge volunteer army. In fact military leaders assumed great powers in most of the countries involved. 'War is the continuation of state policy by other means.' Lloyd George, who had become Prime Minister in December 1916, was appalled by the loss of life. However Haig continued to get his way throughout 1917 and 1918 and Lloyd George never really threatened Haig. In Germany, Ludendorff and Hindenburg reduced the Kaiser to a mere spectator. Conscription was not confined to military service; in Germany a forty-three year age range was pressed into industrial service.

LEFT: David Lloyd George, Prime Minsiter, 1916-1922.

'Total war' in Britain took time to become accepted. There was stringent rationing largely due to U-boat activity, and women took on jobs traditionally done by men. By 1918, one million women alone were involved in engineering work on the factory floor. With Zeppelin raids, shelling from ships and submarine activity everyone was directly affected by war.

Jingoism was rife, every alien was interned, fit-looking men in civilian clothes were presented with white feathers, *ersatz* products appeared on both sides and the British popular papers were keen to elaborate on alleged atrocities 'by the dastardly Hun'. The rape of Belgium, execution of nurse Edith Cavell in 1915, spies dressed up as nuns and soldiers waving white flags before opening fire were all reported. In reality there were atrocities committed on both sides but the allied examples tended to be isolated incidents.

ABOVE: The aftermath of a German bombing raid on London during World War I.

CHAPTER FOURTEEN

1917: the Year of Endurance

J OFFRE HAD BEEN promoted away from the front and the new French Commander was General Nivelle. He was not short on confidence. Things started well, with Nivelle convincing the British politicians and his own officers that his policy of artillery barrage and surprise infantry attack would earn the breakthough. Unfortunately the Germans hadn't been wasting their time. The Hindenburg line was consolidated with a scorched earth policy in the 30km to its front.

Haig and Lloyd George argued long and hard about what could be achieved on the Western Front; another personality clash was between Haig and General Sir Henry Wilson, the Liaison Officer with the French.

LEFT: British troops go into action, spring 1917.

The British attacked on 9 April at Arras, and the French a week later on the Aisne. Nivelle's attack was a disaster. More French were killed than Germans, a maximum 6km had been gained by the end of the month and Nivelle was replaced by Pétain. It was at this point that around thirty-five thousand French troops mutinied. It took the form of refusing to advance when ordered. This was kept from the British and even the French Government were not fully informed. The Germans received the news too late to capitalise on it; fifty-five French men were executed. On a more positive note, the Canadians took Vimy Ridge on 10 April. This chalk eminence was riddled with tunnels and mining operations and pock-marked with shell-holes. The Allies paid another high price; today one can find sixty thousand names on the white, sombre memorial at the crest. Need I add that the attack petered out, and another quarter of a million casualties were added to the ledger? Twenty thousand prisoners did a little to sweeten the Allied pill.

In Russia troops deserted from the front, the Germans made huge gains and the Russians sued for peace as civil war engulfed the nation. The Revolution was critical for the Allies as the Germans could now move most of their forces to the Western Front.

Haig still believed direct frontal assault was the answer. He and Admiral Sir John Jellicoe considered the Germans were near breaking point and a plan to take the Passchendaele Ridge near Ypres and swing north to the ports of Ostend and Zeebrugge appeared feasible. Ypres became the focus and the British, until the end of the war, took on the main burden on the Western Front.

OVERLEAF: British troops of the East Yorkshire regiment at Frezenberg, 5 September 1917.

The Messines Ridge, south of Ypres, had been mined for over a year. No less than nineteen mines exploded in the early hours of 7 June and after the traditional bombardment, a stunning assault achieved almost total success. Two mines failed to explode. One detonated in July 1955 and the other remains east of Ploegsteert Wood. It was a classic piece of siege warfare. This opening to the Third Battle of Ypres was followed up. On 31 July the main assault east of Ypres began. The initial casualties were well down on the appalling figures for the first day of the Somme 1916. However, rain started that afternoon and the pitted surface became a quagmire. Everything began to sink into the mud. Phase Two at Langemark on 16-18 August made little headway.

By 12 October the rain had become a deluge but Haig insisted the British fight on. The Battle of Passchendaele came to symbolise the awful fighting conditions on the Western Front as men slogged up the slopes to the German positions. On 7 November, the Canadians took the village of Passchendaele and the battle ended. Half a million casualties reflect the carnage. Haig's reputation plummeted, the salient became even harder to defend after the fronts settled and there was even a rebellion at the Etaples base camp near Boulogne. The Third Battle of Ypres was the worst waste in a war noted for its criminal use of manpower. A walk around Tyne Cot on the slopes below Passchendaele leaves a lasting impression on those who visit the front. And then there are the thirty-five thousand names on the walls of men who have no known graves.

Ten days after the closure of the Ypres offensive the British attacked at Cambrai, 70km to the south. This countryside was far more conducive

LEFT: Russian soldiers who joined the Russian Revolution of 1917, the Red Flag attached to their bayonets.

to tanks. After a thousand-gun assault, three hundred and eighty-one tanks with infantry moved forward. On a 10km front British troops penetrated over 5km. A 'hurricane' bombardment requiring skilful reliance on maps had proved a success. Nevertheless one hundred and fourteen tanks broke down and sixty-five were knocked out. The infantry failed to keep up and poor communications remained a problem. The British had surprised the Germans with their tanks; the Germans counter-attacked, assisted by skilful aerial observation. The Battle of Cambrai ended on 5 December with around forty-five thousand casualties on both sides and another stalemate.

RIGHT: The Battles of Messines and Third Ypres, June to November, 1917.

OVERLEAF: Battle of Langemarck. Distant shell-bursts near Pilckem. Two R.G.A. men outside their quarters in the remnant of a ruined house, 18 August 1917.

FOLLOWING PAGE: A crowded road at Fricourt, 13 October 1917.

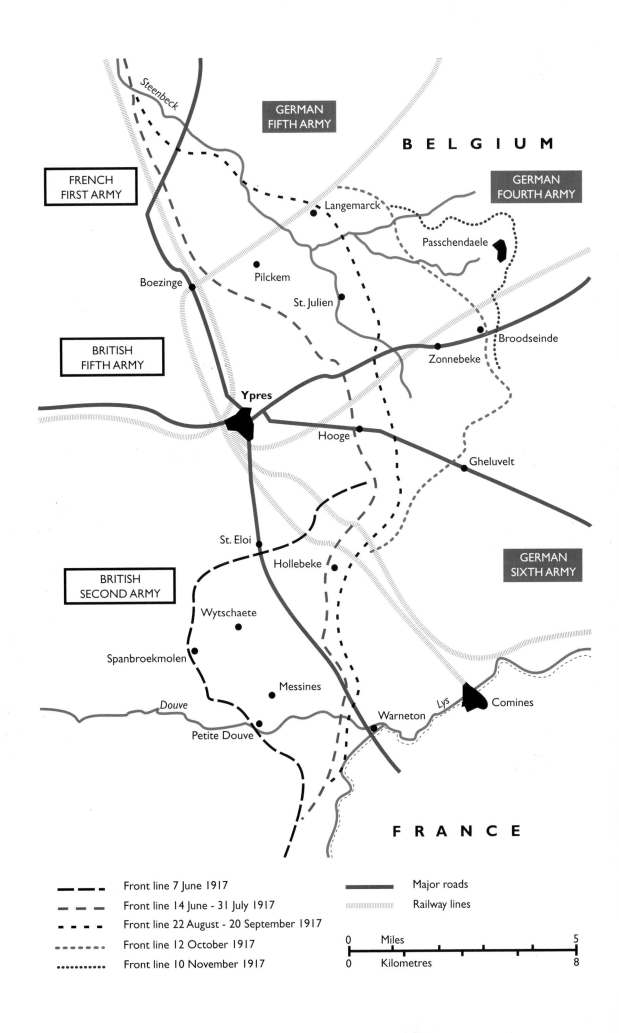

BELGIUM

GERMAN
FIFTH ARMY

GERMAN
FOURTH ARMY

FRENCH
FIRST ARMY

Steenbeck

Langemarck

Passchendaele

Boezinge

Pilckem

St. Julien

Broodseinde

BRITISH
FIFTH ARMY

Zonnebeke

Ypres

Hooge

Gheluvelt

St. Eloi

Hollebeke

GERMAN
SIXTH ARMY

BRITISH
SECOND ARMY

Wytschaete

Spanbroekmolen

Messines

Douve

Lys

Comines

Warneton

Petite Douve

FRANCE

▬ ▬ ▬ Front line 7 June 1917	▬▬▬ Major roads
▬ ▬ ▬ Front line 14 June - 31 July 1917	▓▓▓ Railway lines
▪ ▪ ▪ Front line 22 August - 20 September 1917	
···· Front line 12 October 1917	
•••• Front line 10 November 1917	

0 Miles 5
0 Kilometres 8

LEFT: A wiring party of guards crossing a captured canal.

OVERLEAF: German retreat to the Hindenburg Line. Cyclists passing through the ruined village of Brie, March 1917.

FOLLOWING PAGE: German retreat to the Hindenburg Line. Cycle orderlies under fire in Etreillers, 20 April 1917.

FOLLOWING PAGE: A half submerged tank, near St Julien. 12 October, 1917 during the Battle of Ypres.

CHAPTER FIFTEEN

The Poets

THERE WAS SOMETHING about the nature of trench warfare that moved both officers and men to verse. Was it a way of explaining the inexplicable? Was it a cathartic exercise, or a method of putting thoughts on paper that couldn't be put in letters? Some pieces were vitriolic, others found humour in the macabre, a few reached genuine greatness. Wilfred Owen was one of the best. He fell a week before the Armistice and left us poems such as *Spring Offensive* , *The Sentry, Mental Cases* and the incomparable *Anthem for Doomed Youth*. Titles such as *Poppies in the Corn, No Man's land, To a Ra*t, *A Lark Above the Trenches, Night Raid, Wirers, The Dug-Out* and *The Casualty Clearing Station* remind us that these writers experienced the true horrors of this form of warfare.

LEFT: Battle of Pilckem Ridge. British soldier giving a light to a badly wounded German lying in a ditch, Pilckem, 31 July 1917.

Wilfred Owen (1893-1918)

Anthem for Doomed Youth

What passing-bells for these who die as cattle?

   – Only the monstrous anger of the guns.

  Only the stuttering rifles' rapid rattle

Can patter out their hasty orisons.

No mockeries now for them; no prayers nor bells;

   Nor any voice of mourning save the choirs,

The shrill demented choirs of wailing shells;

   And bugles calling for them from sad shires.

What candles may be held to speed them all?

   Not in the hands of boys, but in their eyes

Shall shine the holy glimmers of goodbyes.

   The pallor of girls' brows shall be their pall;

Their flowers the tenderness of patient minds,

And each slow dusk a drawing-down of blinds.

ABOVE: Wilfred Owen, front row, third from the right, and group.

OVERLEAF: Action of the the Somme Crossings. Gordons in support watching the fighting. They are halted in the open lining a low ridge. Nesle, 24 March 1918. (Stragglers on 20th Division Front).

CHAPTER SIXTEEN

The Fourth and Final Year

1918 WAS A YEAR OF OFFENCES, advances and retreats by both sides, and most sectors were involved in bloody conflict. The state of the armies at the start of the year makes interesting reading. The Germans were soon free to fight on a single front after the Treaty of Brest-Litovsk with Bolshevik Russia in March. Austria-Hungary was crumbling, the Americans were in the war, the British were surviving the submarine activity and the Germans realised a victory was now or never. The Germans were in a hurry and reintroduced the element of surprise. Meanwhile, the French Army was in trouble with falling morale and lack of recruits. The British Army was by now dominated by conscripts and morale was shaky after Passchendaele.

LEFT: The arrival of the first batch of British prisoners captured in German breakthrough at St. Quentin, March 1918.

OVERLEAF: Renault Tank on the road near St Julien, 2 October 1918.

The Germans had 194 Divisions to the 156 of the French and British, and they decided to attack on the Somme. After the usual bombardment, the German infantry advanced on 21 March. Many British prisoners were taken but they retreated under control and Marshal Ferdinand Ludendorff unwisely split his forces into three. With Marshal Foch now in overall control, the Germans were 'pincered' by the British to the north and the French to the south. German discipline began to slip and the Australians halted the enemy advance to Amiens at Villers-Brettoneux. The Germans began to suffer big losses; nearly a quarter of a million over sixteen days.

Ludendorff now turned his attention to Flanders for Phase Two. The aim was to crush the British Army once and for all. Two Territorial Divisions saved the day after the Portuguese Division had been routed.

The British line held, and the attack ended with the first tank versus tank encounter of the war. The Germans had swung south of Ypres and taken Mount Kemmel. Yet five days later Ludendorff called off the battle and this time disillusionment began to spread through the German ranks.

The German Commander now returned to the French for Phase Three and on 27 May, Chemin des Dames, east of Soissons became the target. Within seven days he had reached Château-Thierry; only 80km from Paris. The US Army was involved here for the first time. The fourth push opened on the Marne on 15 July; fifty-two German Divisions took on thirty-three. The French, with a large number of tanks and strong American support, eventually pushed the Germans back across the Marne. The casualty figures were awful yet again; the Germans lost nearly one hundred and forty thousand and the Allies marginally less.

However, the initiative had swung to the Allies and they never surrendered it. Ironically these offences lost Germany the war. The fifth and final drive by the German First and Seventh Armies failed to reach Châlons-sur-Marne. The turning point was on 8 August. The British counter-attacked with over four hundred and fifty tanks and the French and Americans added further pushes through to 12 September. The Americans, acting independently for the first time, overran St Mihiel salient in under twenty-four hours. It was the 'black day of the German Army'; their morale sunk to an all-time low and even Ludendorff realised a German victory was impossible. The Americans had opened their account: they could fight after all.

The Americans were inexperienced but no one doubted their enthusiasm. They were also quick to learn. They began to use native

Indian strategy in their attacks and the quality of their rifle marksmanship was second to none. The Germans called them *Teufelhunde* (devil dogs). The troops included both all-American boys and those born in European countries, as well as black servicemen who experienced considerable discrimination. Their Commander-in-Chief, General Pershing, had taken over the St Mihiel sector which had been something of a backwater. Fifteen thousand prisoners were taken at St Mihiel and it was the battle where Patton and MacArthur cut their teeth. The US had entered the war with two hundred thousand men, four hundred heavy guns, fifty planes, no tanks and one song, *Over There*. Back home, innocent dachshunds were being stoned in the streets and Potsdam in Missouri was renamed Pershing.

OVERLEAF: The German Offensive. German reserves marching forward along Albert Road, March 1918.

Foch decided to attack along a wide front to finally drive the Germans back. Attacks at Ypres, the Somme, Aisne and Meuse-Argonne on 26 September lead to the Hindeburg line falling on 4 October. By late September, the northern forces had advanced to the Schelde and in the centre Le Cateau fell on 17 October. It was at this point that Adolf Hitler was gassed near Ypres. The Americans reached Sedan on 10 November. The following day Mons was taken and at 11am the guns fell silent for good.

The Americans had their share of heroes. Air-ace Eddie Rickenbacker had twenty-six 'kills' to his name, and Sergeant Alvin C. York of Tennessee, a conscientious objector-turned-combatant, who on 18 October 1918 killed twenty enemy and captured one hundred and thirty more.

ABOVE: Ludendorff.

OVERLEAF: A pigeon being released from a porthole in the side of a tank, Albert, 1918. During World War I, pigeons were frequently used to carry messages from tanks.

FOLLOWING PAGE: British troops walking through Chateau Wood, Ypres, 29 October 1917.

FOLLOWING PAGE: German prisoners captured in the Battle of the Canal du Nord in a cage near Bapaume, 28 September 1918.

CHAPTER SEVENTEEN

'Only the Dead have Seen an End to War'

Plato

JUST NORTH OF POPERINGHE close to the French/Belgian border lie three British cemeteries named Bandaghem, Mendinghem and Dozinghem. It doesn't take much imagination to work out what the Tommies called these places, which were originally casualty-clearing stations. Those not so lucky may have an individual headstone; if lost in the mud or blown to pieces their names will appear on such moving memorials as the Menin Gate and Thiepval. Only a day's drive around the Ypres Salient or the Somme, passing endless 'silent cities' really gives a sense of the enormity of the conflict. One of the saddest stones lies alongside the road from Arras to Doullens. 10495 Private Albert

LEFT: A German war cemetery containing five thousand graves at Sailly-sur-la-Lys, 12 October 1918.

Ingham, 18th Battalion, Manchester Regiment; 1 December 1916. 'Shot at dawn. One of the first to enlist. A worthy son of his father.' There is a school of thought that believes some of these executions were 'pour encourager les autres'. Over three hundred British soldiers were executed. Germany, with a far bigger army, executed less than twenty.

It seemed a sensible idea to put together men from the same street, club or factory. The Pals' Regiments were good for morale at the front but devastating for those at home after 'a big push'. The Accrington Pals' and Chorley Pals' memorials in the Serre area at the north end of the 1916 Somme advance bear witness to this.

31939 Corporal R. Lee (RFA) and 6029 Sergeant G. Lee (RFA) lie side by side in Dartmoor cemetery on the Somme. They died on 5 September 1916, aged 19 and 44 respectively; father and son serving on the same gun. Brothers Private P.J. Destrube, 26, and Lance Corporal C.G. Destrube, 27, of the Royal Fusiliers, killed in the Ypres Salient on 17 February 1917 share the same parents and headstone. Lieutenant Henry Webber, South Lancashire Regiment, killed 21 July 1916 aged 68 and Private W.W. Speight, Royal Welch Fusiliers, 11 August 1917 aged 62 are two of the oldest British casualties.

What can one say about the following?

Private J. Condon, Royal Irish Regiment, 24 May 1915
Poelkapelle Cemetery, aged 14

Rifleman V.J. Strudwick, The Rifle Brigade, 14 January 1916
Essex Farm Cemetery, aged 15

Private A.E. French, 18th Btn KRRC, 15 June 1916
Hyde Park Corner Cemetery, aged 16

'Their names liveth for evermore'

ABOVE: German postcard, which says 'Fallen English', shows dead Scottish soldiers.

CHAPTER EIGHTEEN

The Aftermath

11 NOVEMBER SAW scenes in London and Paris that many would find extraordinary, even today. After three days the police in London had to clear the streets. In Moscow the Bolsheviks expected communist revolution to sweep across Europe. 'Make Germany pay' was the common cry; the Allies believed they had been fighting for a noble cause. Soldiers were restless to return home. German soldiers felt stabbed in the back and tens of thousands drifted away from the retreating columns to return home. The Allies were exhausted, the Americans stopped their loans immediately, the question of the severity of the peace deal had to be tackled and what should be done with the Bolsheviks?

LEFT: Crowds celebrating armistice day outside Buckingham Palace. The British Royal family watched from the balcony.

In January 1919 Lloyd George, Wilson, Clemenceau (The big Three) and Orlando met in Paris. They jumped from issue to issue and returned home on several occasions. They all believed a League of Nations was the answer but all had different views on its role. German colonies were to be carved up, the British wanted the German navy destroyed, the German blockade continued and the view persisted in many quarters that there was 'no such thing as a good German'. Alsace-Lorraine was returned to France, Danzig became a Free City, Austria and Germany were forced to remain separate, Germany was disarmed and they would pay reparations as part of a 'war guilt' clause. Germany signed the treaty in June 1919 but felt it to be totally unfair and punitive.

Bulgaria, Germany, Austria-Hungary and Russia all lost vast tracts of land. The Rhineland became a zone of Allied occupation and plebiscite areas such as the Saarland and Silesia were ceded or retained by the League of Nations. Russia was driven into isolation; two worlds had been created. France and Germany had lost around four and a half and six and a half million men respectively. The British Empire lost over three million and Russia probably ten million. USA casualties numbered three hundred and twenty six thousand. Destruction had been concentrated in a relatively small area and it was extraordinary how quickly the economies of the West got into shape again. Monarchies and European Empires had been culled. The USA retreated into isolation; pacificism spread within Britain and the French built the Maginot line. Germany festered as her Army had been told to lay down its arms on foreign soil.

Women over thirty were enfranchised in Britain in 1918. Only three of the English Rugby Football team survived to play Wales in 1920. J.F. Greenwood was still down as Cambridge University in the programme. The German fleet was scuttled in Scarpa Flow. America was confirmed as a superpower politically, economically and militarily. A united Ireland only lasted a further four years.

After man had done his best to wipe out a generation, nature took its turn in the winter of 1918. An explosion of a new kind, Spanish flu, killed an estimated forty million people worldwide. Fifteen years later Adolf Hitler came to power, and six years after that the countries of Europe were at each others' throats again.

RIGHT: The Versailles Conference Armistice Talks, 1918.

ABOVE: Adolf Hitler, left in the front row with drooping moustache.

RIGHT: Hitler on the far right of the picture, who never rose above the rank of corporal.

FURTHER READING

FOR GENERAL READING: *History of the 20th Century: WW1 1914-1918,*
Equinox Books (Hamlyn Edition) © J.M. Winter 1988
ISBN 0600 57990 5
FOR MORE SPECIALISED READING: *The First Day of the Somme*
Martin Middlebrook, Allen Lane, The Penguin Press, 1971,
ISBN 07139 0194 2
Somme Lyn Macdonald, Papermac, Macmillan, 1983,
ISBN 0333 366484
They Called It Passchendaele Lyn Macdonald, Michael Joseph,
London, 1978, ISBN 07181 1735 2

ACKNOWLEDGEMENTS

IMPERIAL WAR MUSEUM: Page 16/17: q42033, page 24: q716,
page 28/29: q32003, page 30/31: q56522, page 32: q30505,
page 36: q10681, page 42/43: q1582, page 46/47: q3990,
page 48/49: q8430, page 50: q5817, page 54: q5937,
page 56/57 q49082, page 58: q49094, page 62/63: co29999,
page 64/65: q11586, page 69: q17688, page 70: q49104,
page :74/75: q669, page 80/81: q20220, page 82: q19159,
page 84: q23934, page 90: q5574, page 92: q1321, page 94: q2041,
page 106/107 q56530, page 108/109 q70167, page 110 q55066,
page 112 q58028, page115: q68244, page 116/117: q12121,
page 122: q5100, page 126/127 q3014, page 134/135 q2734,
page 136/137 q5794, page 140/141: q1868, page 142/143 q2098,
page 144/145 q6327, page 146: q2629, page 149: q71250,
page 150/151 q10785.

All other pictures courtesy of the Illustrated London News and
collection of the author. Text on pages 41, 44 and 45 © The Times
Newspaper Ltd, 1993.